the new book of

Table Settings

creative ideas for the way we gather today

D1362157

the new book of

Table Settings

creative ideas for the way we gather today

chris bryant

paige gilchrist

LARK BOOKS

A Division of
Sterling Publishing Co., Inc
New York

PAIGE GILCHRIST
editor

CHRIS BRYANT
art director

SKIP WADE
creative coordinator,
props, stylist

EVAN BRACKEN
photography

THOM GAINES
illustrations

**CATHARINE SUTHERLAND
HEATHER SMITH**
editorial assistance

HANNES CHAREN
production assistance

SPECIAL PHOTOGRAPHY
Dennis Brandsma, pg. 120
Peter Kooijman, pg. 68
Dolf Straatemeier, pg. 84
George v.d. Wijngaard,
    pp. 88 and 99
Hans Zeegers, pg. 64

Library of Congress Cataloging-in-Publication Data

Gilchrist, Paige.
    The new book of table settings : creative ideas for the way we gather today / Chris
Bryant, art director ; Paige Gilchrist.
        p. cm.
    ISBN 157990-255-3
    1. Table setting and decoration. 2. Table etiquette. I. Bryant, Chris. II. Title.

TX871 .G55 2000
642'.6--dc21

                                                                                        00-035227

10 9 8 7 6 5 4 3 2 1

Published by Lark Books,
a division of Sterling Publishing Co., Inc.
387 Park Avenue South
New York, N.Y. 10016

First Paperback Edition 2001
© 2000, Lark Books

Distributed in Canada by Sterling Publishing,
c/o Canadian Manda Group, One Atlantic Ave., Suite 105
Toronto, Ontario, Canada M6K 3E7

Distributed in the U.K. by Guild of Master Craftsman Publications Ltd.
Castle Place, 166 High Street, Lewes, East Sussex, England BN7 1XU
Tel: (+ 44) 1273 477374, Fax: (+ 44) 1273 478606
Email: pubs@thegmcgroup.com, Web: www.gmcpublications.com

Distributed in Australia by Capricorn Link (Australia) Pty Ltd.
P.O. Box 704, Windsor, NSW 2756 Australia

If you have questions or comments about this book, please contact:
Lark Books
67 Broadway
Asheville, North Carolina 28801
(828) 253-0467

Printed in China

ISBN 1-57990-255-3

contents

8 introduction

10 the basics

38 food is the focus

58 available in season

84 nontraditional table

106 a reason to celebrate

126 contributing consultants

127 acknowledgments

128 index

S ETTING A TABLE IS LIKE RUNNING OR GETTING A GOOD night's sleep. You did a lot of it as a child, so you felt perfectly qualified to tackle it as an adult. Until you started hearing about how hard it is to get it right. Suddenly, you were aware of intricate rules of etiquette, elaborate gadgetry, and a minefield of potential problems. Before you knew it, you were certain that without expert advice and a bunch of expensive paraphernalia, you could do a great deal of damage (or at the very least fail) if you attempted it.

Nonsense.

Welcoming others to our tables is an instinct that's both universal and ages old. Making those tables inviting places to share good food and good company is a natural inclination, not an esoteric art. In other words, you can still do this. With the dishes (and candleholders and vases and other accessories) you already own, for the most part. And with innovative, creative touches that don't take more time to prepare than the meal. We've put together a book that shows you how.

First, we give you solid grounding in the basics; we provide an overview of the components of a standard table setting and primers on traditional protocol (which fork goes where and so on). The idea here is not strict instruction, but easy reference—and a jumping off point for improvisation. Then, improvise we do, through page after page of beautiful settings for sharing food, drink, and conversation. We think you'll find them imaginative and full of inspiration. But most of all, we think you'll find them do-able—that you'll see them as settings that can be recreated on real tables, in real homes, with pieces pulled from the cabinets and cupboards of real people. Which is probably because that's exactly where these settings started.

introduction

We created the majority of the table settings in this book in our own homes and those of friends. Most feature our own dinnerware, flatware, and the rest, supplemented by pieces borrowed from friends and family; other pieces we used are from thrift stores and antique shops. Only a few are new purchases from stores that sell housewares and home accessories. Many of the settings are developed around an all-purpose collection of standard tableware (easy and inexpensive to assemble; you probably already own most of what you'll need). That means you don't have to invest in several new sets of designer dishes to translate the looks to your own table.

And every design is based on the idea that the ways we cook, eat, and entertain today are different from what they once were. In an era when takeout in front of the fireplace counts as having friends over for dinner and a potluck picnic is far more common than a five-course meal, styles are more relaxed and settings can often be much more casual. We offer a simple, uncomplicated approach that fits the times. Our settings typically focus on one interesting idea (or great color or clever solution to a serving problem) rather than a lot of competing decoration. They draw on the everyday for inspiration (from the changing seasons to the challenges of entertaining a crowd) and incorporate ordinary, accessible items into distinctive displays.

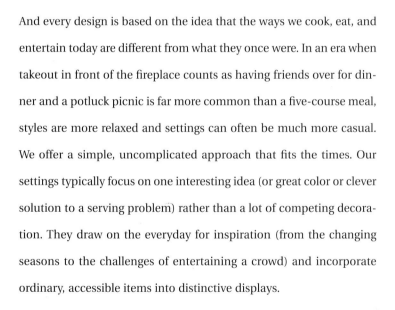

So pull up a chair, flip through the following pages, and remind yourself how much you already know about making a table a welcoming place. Then, put the book aside and do what comes naturally—invite someone to sit down and join you.

the basics

the basics

In this chapter we bring to the table, so to speak, the five basic components of a setting: dinnerware, glassware, flatware, linens, and decorative elements. Of course, you won't use all five every time you sit down to eat. (Let's face it, in the imperfect world of reality, many of us create most of our "settings" by picking a plate from the top of the stack, grabbing whatever silverware is clean, ripping a paper towel from the roll, and heading for the couch.) But when you get the urge to do it right, it's nice to know how to pull it off.

We take you on a visual tour of the table-settings universe. Plates come in everything from fine china to rustic stoneware, for example. You can drink out of cut-glass goblets, brightly colored plastic tumblers, or earthenware mugs. Flatware can take the form of honest-to-goodness silver or stainless steel with Lucite handles (and lots in between), and linens don't always have to be linen. We offer all the options for changing the look and mood of your table.

Then, imagining that you, too, have a finite amount of space in your kitchen cabinets and limits to your tableware budget, we show you how to put together a basic, neutral collection that provides a foundation for a wide array of settings. Throughout the rest of the book, we use just such a collection, showing you how to expand and embellish it with accent pieces to create as many settings as you can imagine.

speaking of doing it right...

Some of society's most complex rules have to do with the proper way to serve, share, and eat food. No wonder few of us are ever fully confident we're getting it right. (Do we pick it up, do we use a fork—and which fork, for crying out loud?) Early in our eating careers, we heard that etiquette books held the answers, but many were so full of highbrow shushes and scolding that they intimidated more often than they helped.

Let us offer some words to relax by. If you look beneath most etiquette-book do's and don'ts, you'll find a foundation of logic, practicality, and common sense. Most of the table-related customs we now think of as rules came about not to intimidate the uninitiated, but to help meals run smoothly, to enhance the food and drink, and to make both guests and hosts comfortable. Who could argue with those good intentions? They're as suited to a modern-day potluck as they were to a banquet a century ago.

What *has* changed is how creatively many hosts now carry out the rules. As with most things in life, it's easier to improvise with success (not to mention flair) if you have a grip on the time-tested basics first. In that spirit, we've provided a running primer on traditional table-setting etiquette. Use it to lay down a nice table, as a point of departure for an approach more suited to how you entertain today—or as interesting trivia to spark lively dinner conversation!

FACING PAGE: A basic collection of table-setting components. These standard, neutural pieces can provide the foundation for a wide variety of settings.

dinnerware

LIKE INTERESTING CONVERSATION AND GOOD food, dinnerware helps form the foundation of a successful meal. And just like the talk and the food, dinnerware can range from quiet to boisterous, familiar to exotic. With so many styles to choose from, here's something nice to know: you don't have to settle on just one. Mixing and matching different dinnerware is one of the best ways to set a creative table.

Let's say you have a set of basic white dinnerware. (And we recommend you do; more about that later.) You're using it to set the table for a dinner to celebrate the coming of spring. On one white dinner plate, you place a translucent green glass salad plate. Very pretty, eh? Look how nice the white plate looks through the pale green glass. Now, on top of the green, you add a pink china soup bowl. (Hey, it's a big meal, okay? Just go with it.) Not enough pink bowls to go around? Then at every other place, use a yellow bowl, or a blue one. It'll be lovely—only more springy.

Even if it's the dead of winter where you are now and you hate pastel dishes, you get the point. Playing around with a mix of colors, textures, and styles of dinnerware can help you come up with a wonderfully creative table setting. (You don't have to own all of these colors, textures, and styles, by the way. Borrowing dishes from family and friends is a tradition as time-honored as exchanging recipes. Of course, you probably should invite them to dinner if you're serving it on their plates.)

IN *the 18th century, most ceramics were imported from China. Hence, the name we still use today for fine ceramic dinnerware, which typically falls into one of four categories: earthenware, stoneware, porcelain, or bone china.*

ABOVE: Basic white dinnerware is hard to beat if you're after a classic, elegant look.

RIGHT: Dinnerware comes in glass, too, which coordinates wonderfully with a basic white set.

dinnerware basics

Over time, try to piece together a set of basic white dinnerware. Not everything has to be the same style, just match the shades of white as closely as possible. Try for ten dinner plates, soup plates (shallow wide bowls as opposed to the deeper cereal bowls), smaller luncheon or salad plates, and dessert plates.

You can find plain white dinnerware at kitchen-supply stores, department stores, discount retailers, even thrift stores. It often ranks among the least expensive. Search for simple, classic designs; avoid unusual or trendy looks. You're after a versatile set that will last.

Did we mention that white goes with just about everything? You can pair it with a variety of tablecloths, napkins, and glassware for surprisingly different effects. As for the food you're serving, almost everything—especially brightly colored food—looks best on white dishes.

Once you've got a white foundation, you can begin to play with color and pattern. For example, collect small sets of key dishes—dinner plates, salad plates, soup bowls—in colors you like. Paired with your basic whites, just a few accent pieces can provide the variety you need to change the mood of your table from meal to meal.

TOP: Clear glass plates are perfect for a light spring luncheon. A larger white dinnerplate is used underneath as a service plate.

CENTER: Shallow soup bowls also make excellent salad bowls for serving bigger, heartier salads.

BOTTOM: You don't have to own a complete set of lavender dinnerware to infuse your setting with a dramatic bit of color. For this setting, we combined the dinner plates with clear salad plates and bowls.

according to etiquette

■ For formal dinners, a service plate (a decorative plate larger than the dinner plate) is placed at each setting. It remains on the table for the first course or two to protect table linens and showcase smaller pieces of dinnerware; the appetizer plate and soup bowl are set on top of it. The service plate is always removed before the main course.

■ Traditionally, plates for any one course match each other, though patterns and styles may vary throughout the meal. But confident hosts mix and match freely.

■ Most soups are served in wide, shallow bowls with broad rims. Consommés and cream soups, however, may be served in small, deep bowls. Proper consommé bowls, looking like two-handled teacups, are made to be lifted and sipped from and are used only for clear soups.

■ Salad plates and cups and saucers are never set in advance, but are brought to the table as needed.

■ Europeans feel butter plates have no place at formal dinners. Bread (usually hard-crusted rolls) should be eaten unbuttered and placed directly on the tablecloth to the left of the plate. If you opt for butter plates, place them at the upper left of each place setting.

■ Finger bowls are shallow, rimless glass or silver bowls filled with tepid water and a lemon slice (especially if seafood is being served) or a scented geranium leaf or rose petal or herb. They can be brought to the table on dessert plates, with the dessert fork and spoon resting on either side of the bowl. Guests remove the fork and spoon (placing them to either side of the plate) and place the finger bowl at the upper left of the setting, opposite the water glass. Finger bowls may also be set, saucer or not, to the left of each diner's plate after the appropriate course has been cleared. Guests dip their fingertips only, then dab them on a napkin.

■ Entrées should be served on hot plates (unless it's a cold summertime meal). To heat them, place them on the rack in a 175°F (80°C) oven for about 15 minutes, then remove them with a potholder. Or, use the drying cycle of a dishwasher or run them under hot tap water.

glassware

A FEW THOUSAND YEARS AGO, WE HUMANS learned how to fuse sand and soda with fire to form glass. It's been a prized package of contradictions since: fragile yet strong, liquid yet solid, the stuff of both skyscrapers and jewels. And, of course, of glistening drinking vessels that bring a table to life.

Glassware is often the most sparkling element you add to a table. Mix the sparkle factor of glass with candlelight, and the result is an enchanting backdrop to your meal. Dinners of multiple courses accompanied by several types of wine offer the best opportunities for creating the effect. Etiquette tells us we can place up to three wineglasses plus a water goblet at each setting. That's quite a bit of sparkle.

Sounds dazzling, you're thinking, *but I'll never be able to collect enough matching crystal for that.* Who said anything about matching crystal? Or any crystal? If your glasses match (and they're crystal), great. If they don't (and they aren't), that's often even more interesting. Use any collection of stemware you've got for white wineglasses. Water glasses can be generic, straight-sided tumblers, red wine can be served Italian-style in short juice glasses, and cordials after dinner can go in any small, mismatched glasses (shot glasses work especially well). Varying heights, mixing colors, and mingling everything from antique cut glass to modern geometric designs adds to the interest of the table setting—and it's often the most practical way to pull together all the glassware you need.

LEFT: Many consider lead crystal to be glass at its finest, both because of the way it feels and how it collects and reflects light. Still, there are lots of other options.

glassware basics

As with standard white dinnerware, plain clear glasses are best if you want a versatile collection of basics. We're certainly not discouraging you from buying colored glassware; it's stunning on a table. But if you're looking for a foundation, start with clear, then add colored pieces for accents later. You can build your collection inexpensively by keeping an eye out for different types of everyday glasses at thrift stores, yard sales, and kitchen-supply store sale tables.

TOP OF PAGE: A selection of everyday glassware

ABOVE: Even when not from a matched set, most glassware works well together if the pieces share a similar color cast.

according to etiquette

■ Wine and water glasses are set before the meal, with no more than three wineglasses set at a time (even if more wines are being served).

■ The main-course wineglass is placed approximately ½ inch (1.3 cm) above the point of the main-course knife. All others are arranged on a northwestern to southeastern diagonal from this point, according to when they will be used.

■ Separate glasses for red and white wine dress up a setting, but are not essential. A good-sized glass with a rounded, somewhat elongated bowl and a rim that is narrower than the bowl is best if you're using only one.

■ Water goblets should hold more than wineglasses. They're also more rounded and flatter where the bowl meets the stem.

■ The water goblet is placed above all the wineglasses, closest to the inside of the table.

■ A tall tumbler for iced tea or lemonade in lieu of wine goes where the main-course wineglass would otherwise sit.

■ Wine (like all drinks) is poured from the right. Better for a host to hold the bottle near the guest's glass and ask, *May I?*, than to query from across the table, *Would you like some more wine?*

■ Crystal should be impeccably spotless. Each glass should be wiped with a lint-free cotton or linen cloth before being placed on the table by its stem.

■ Wine coasters are recommended to keep dripping wine from decorating the tablecloth.

TOP-LEFT: Two different styles of champagne flutes paired with deep red water goblets.

CENTER-LEFT: Although markedly different, the styles and sizes of these glasses complement each other splendidly.

LEFT: Glasses are not always glass! Here is a selection of plastic and metal drinking vessels.

flatware

RULES GOVERNING FLEETS OF FORKS, KNIVES, spoons, and other utensils blossomed during the Victorian era. That's when those in the classiest classes had time to focus on the accessories of life, money to obtain them, and servants to handle the details of setting tables with everything from jelly trowels and aspic knives to pickle forks and individual asparagus tongs. Today, you can lay a striking (and perfectly acceptable) setting with no more utensils than forks. And if you thought sterling silver was required, read on.

Here's a news flash: most people have mismatched sets of flatware. Open any kitchen "silverware" drawer, and you'll usually find a hodgepodge of family hand-me-downs, incomplete collections from college house-sharing days, and a few strange strays that mysteriously found a home there. It's typically a mix of colorful Lucite handles, a few silver-plated pieces, and lots of stainless steel.

Though it's difficult to make a coherent table setting out of a completely random collection of flatware, you don't have to start from scratch to come up with what you need. Many people with full sets of flatware actually have blended families. (Grandma's rose pattern gets mixed with the rose pattern available when mom was married. They are so compatible, and have been keeping house together so long, they almost look alike.) The key is to strategically match as you mix pieces.

flatware basics

No surprise, plain and unobtrusive are best if you want an all-purpose set of flatware. Stay away from colored handles, gold-plating, and unusual designs if you're after a set that will go with everything. Simple, silver-colored pieces are at home in most any setting.

GETTING THAT BASIC SILVER COLOR

Sterling silver is the real thing. It can also be a lot of work. If you want shiny forks and knives that never need polishing and expect to throw your flatware in the dishwasher after you've used it, sterling silver isn't going to meet your daily needs.

Silver-plated flatware is just what it sounds like: a metal base with a silver plate. It's graded by how many times it's been plated (single, double, or triple plate). Silver plate is less expensive than sterling silver, but it's still going to keep you busy polishing and hand washing.

Stainless steel flatware is nearly effortless to care for, and it comes in styles ranging from American Colonial to sleek and modern, flowery to wildly eccentric. Look for heavy stainless steel, and avoid cheap flatware with thin handles. The poor-quality stuff has little chance of surviving that inevitable encounter with the garbage disposal—not to mention the other pressures of everyday life.

Many antique, secondhand, and consignment stores sell silver and silver-plated flatware. Most good restaurant and hotel silver is triple plated, and if you can find it, it makes a durable utensil good for everyday use. (Hotel silver is especially in demand, because the pieces are often larger and more contemporary looking.) If you've got an incomplete set of silver or silver plate and want to fill it out, you're in luck. Many shapes and designs are similar from pattern to pattern. It's easy to mix and match with pieces that complement each other.

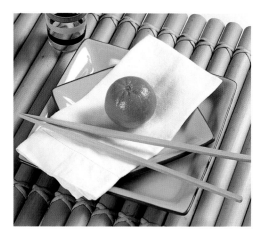

TOP: A flatware design with a contemporary twist

CENTER: Simple flatware (stainless)

BOTTOM: If you're setting your table with chopsticks, be sure to have forks, knives, and spoons available for those who prefer them.

according to etiquette

■ Set flatware so that guests can confidently work from the outside in when choosing which implement to use: forks to the left of the plate, knives (blades facing in) to the right, and spoons to the right of the knives.

■ Exceptions: Seafood forks (for first-course clams, oysters, etc., not to be confused with fish forks) are placed on the right, outside the knives and spoons. For settings with no knives (such as a simple salad meal), the fork is placed on the right by itself or on the right inside the spoon (if the setting also includes a soup spoon, for example).

■ After each course, remove the accompanying flatware.

■ Europeans often set forks with the tines down, creating what they feel is a more handsome appearance.

■ The French sometimes add to each setting a porte-couteau or knife rest—a small bar, usually of silver or glass, for resting the blade of a "sauce-streaked" knife. They also frequently set sauce spoons (with nearly flattened bowls), which allow more graceful scooping of sauce as opposed to sopping it up with bread.

■ Dessert implements go above the plate. The fork points right, the spoon left, as if each were simply moved up from its position beside the plate.

■ Beverage spoons (such as those for iced tea) go to the right of all the other implements. Coffee spoons go to the far right, too, or, most often, are served on the saucer with the coffee.

■ Butter knives are placed on each butter plate, in a position that mirrors that of the main-course knife.

■ Steak knives should be an addition to (not replacement for) main-course knives.

■ Set no more flatware beside each plate than is required for three courses (plus dessert pieces above the plate). If four or more non-dessert courses are to be served, deliver new flatware after the first three.

■ Salad forks and luncheon knives are suitable substitutes for fish forks (squat and thick tined) and fish knives (elongated and trowel shaped, suitable for filleting small fish at the table).

■ Unless you know that your guests prefer them, set chopsticks in addition to, not instead of, other flatware. Place them to the right of the outermost spoon.

ACCEPTABLE FINGER FOODS:

• Fried chicken

• French fries and onion rings

• Small fowl and game birds

• Corn on the cob

• Spare ribs

• Crab

• Lobster still in their shells

• Asparagus without sauce

a. mustard spoon
b. sauce ladle
c. cream ladle
d. gravy ladle
e. berry spoon

f. cream soup spoon (indiv.)
g. sugar spoon
h. jelly spoon
i. orange spoon (indiv.)
j. sugar tongs

k. ice tongs
l. fish fork (indiv.)
m. kraut or lettuce fork
n. pickle fork
o. lemon fork

p. ice cream trowel
q. jelly server
r. rice or vegetable server
s. jelly server
t. vegetable fork

u. cold meat fork
v. cold meat fork
w. demitasse spoon
x. demitasse spoon
y. salt spoon

napkins &
table coverings

S O, YOU FORGOT TO PACK A HOPE CHEST FULL OF MONOGRAMMED
damask and tea-dipped antique lace. Good thing times have changed.
Heirloom linen is still in, but now, so are splashy colors, supple fabrics, exotic textures, and bold patterns. What's more, everything from cotton sheets to Indian saris can double as tablecloths, scarves can serve as
runners, and one-of-a-kind napkins can be clipped from a favorite bolt of
cloth. Come to think of it, who needs a prepacked chest anyway?

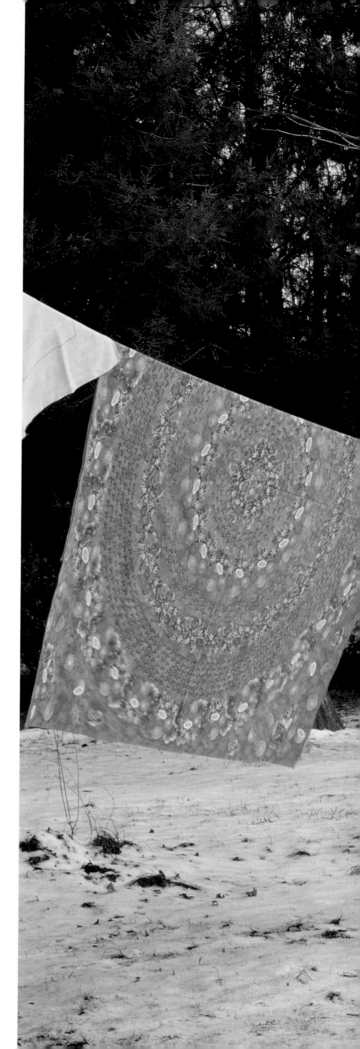

EW TABLE-SETTING COMPONENTS ARE AS easy to come up with as tablecloths. Sure, you can buy them ready made in a wide range of colors and patterns. But you can also quickly create originals when you see tablecloths for what they really are: big pieces of fabric. With so many kinds and colors of fabric available today (and with most tablecloths requiring only a couple of yards [meters]), you can change the look of your table completely for very little money and effort. Buy what you like, then hem the ends or not, depending on how formal a look you're after.

Like tablecloths, napkins are just squares of fabric, so they're easy to whip up if you don't have exactly the shade or style you need. A yard (.9 m) of fabric yields four standard-sized napkins. Simply cut the piece into quarters, then either hem each of the edges or apply fusible web. If your enthusiasm exceeds your sewing ability, adopt the raveled look by removing a few rows of threads on each edge of the cut fabric.

TABLECLOTH TIP

Vintage fabrics are especially popular today—and they make terrific tablecloths. (Think big florals from the 1940s, '50s-modern prints, and pale pastels from the early 1960s.) You can find fabrics like these everywhere from yard sales to antique and consignment stores.

napkin & table-covering basics

Here we are again, touting the importance of a couple of basic pieces. For table linens, we recommend a simple, good-quality, white cotton tablecloth and heavy white cotton napkins. They're just plain practical. They match just about everything, and if you spill food on them (highly likely, wouldn't you say?) you can bleach them back to bright white—even red wine comes out with bleach. Heavy cotton is essential, though, especially for the napkins; bleach can be hard on fabric.

Your trusty white tablecloth is also an indispensable "undergarment." Most of the interesting fabrics we were telling you about earlier are fairly thin. Thin fabric makes a poor tablecloth; it doesn't dampen the clinking of plates, silverware, and glasses the way a thicker cloth does, and it doesn't feel as sturdy. But a basic white cloth underneath makes thin fabric work. A white underlayer also sets off gauzy, translucent, and iridescent fabrics, making their colors pop. A white cotton bed sheet, folded and doubled, serves as a fine undergarment, too.

A CASE FOR CLOTH

With today's focus on recycling and conservation, cloth napkins have even more going for them than style. It's not unthinkable to use them every day, for every meal. And if the specter of laundry baskets teeming with cloth napkins scares you, practice a popular Italian custom. Give each family member his or her own cloth napkin, to be used for every meal. (They hang on the backs of the chairs at the table or on a special rack in the kitchen or dining room in between.) If you really get into the spirit, embroider individual initials on the corners of each napkin, so everyone is sure whose is whose. All that's left is setting up a schedule for rotating in clean napkins on a regular basis.

TOP: Simple white napkins

CENTER: Layering thin transluscent fabric on a thicker base cloth creates rich color. The thicker cloth also helps muffle the clincking of tableware.

BOTTOM: These over-sized, monogrammed napkins are beautiful draped on the backs of chairs.

TOP: Wooden table with a small cloth laid diagonally in the center

CENTER: Napkins are an ideal (not to mention easy and inexpensive) way to play up the theme of a meal.

BOTTOM: The center of the plate can be just the place to set a simply folded napkin and a few utensils.

napkins & table-coverings according to etiquette

■ A tablecloth is most appropriate for formal meals.

■ Place mats are best on wooden tables (newly polished with odorless wax).

■ Cotton or linen napkins (spotless and pressed smooth) are preferable. Polyester and other artificial fabrics are less absorbent—and less pleasant to the touch. They classically range from the size of a lap (16 to 20 inches [40 to 50 cm] square) to the size of a bed pillow (for quite formal occasions).

■ Leave elaborate, fanciful napkin folding to four-star restaurants. Fold yours in quarters and then in half in rectangles, with the exposed corners facing the bottom left, making it easy for seated eaters to pick them up by one corner, let them drop and unfold completely, and place them in their laps. Napkins folded in quarters and then triangles and placed atop the plates are also simple and elegant.

■ Folds or creases in tablecloths are acceptable as long as they run the length of the table.

■ Tablecloths may have an 18-inch (45 cm) over-hang, a length which falls gracefully, yet doesn't interfere with the legs of diners.

flowers, candles & centerpieces

NOTHING AGAINST ALL THE STEMWARE AND LINENS. No offense to the plates, utensils, and other essential pieces. But a few of us patiently work our way through assembling and arranging everything else simply because we love the finishing touches. (Truth be told, more than a few of us actually start at this icing-on-the-cake stage—running a dazzling row of pillar candles down the center of the table, filling a vase with just the right mix of wildflowers—then working on the rest from there.) No question about it, this is definitely the fun part.

The simple collection of components we've suggested (neutral-colored dinnerware, clear glassware, and the rest) gives you the perfect canvas. Now the focus is on bringing the picture to life with flowers, candles, interesting centerpieces, and other accents.

Once upon a time, putting the finishing touches on a table was a pretty orthodox activity. Two silver candlesticks, tall white tapers, a purchased floral arrangement, and the look was complete, whether it was summer or winter, daytime or evening. As you flip through this book, you'll notice that times have definitely changed.

Today, your table settings can take their cue from the everyday world around you—and grow more naturally out of the spirit of your event. The changing seasons, the holidays they bring, the food you'll be serving, even the location of your table (whether it's a picnic table outside or a side table near the fireplace) can all provide inspiration. We'll show you how in detail throughout the book. We'll also show you how to use what's within easy reach to carry out what you have in mind—everything from flowering herbs and bare branches to garden urns and toy trucks. It's likely the backyard, the potting shed, the toy box, or the produce aisle of the grocery store will have just what you need to transform your bare canvas into a beautiful setting.

Gather inspiration for centerpieces from sources as diverse as the season you're celebrating (TOP), natural materials (CENTER), and collections of trinkets and knicknacks (BOTTOM).

flower, candle & centerpiece basics

As with all the other components of a table setting, embellishment is easiest if you have some standard supplies.

■ You need a small assortment of vases in a variety of shapes and sizes. Neutral colors (clear, silver, or white) and simple designs are best. If you opt for more distinctive pieces, you'll need a larger collection of colors and styles to meet all your needs.

■ Large urn-shaped vases are especially useful, because they can serve so many functions. Think of them as decorative vessels to hold arrangements of evergreen cones, fruit, or ornaments. Turn them into hurricane-like candle holders. Or use them as sturdy vases for dramatic, long-stemmed flowers and branches.

■ Flowers arranged in vases sometime need help staying put. "Frog" is the clever name for the cage-shaped or tine-covered metal pieces that sit, frog-like, in the bottom of vases to hold stems in place. And, like real frogs, they come in a variety of sizes and shapes. A few blocks of green floral foam are also useful for holding flowers in place, especially in spare, Japanese-style arrangements. Glass marbles, available by the bag from craft- and floral-supply stores, do the job, too. Of course, clear marbles are the most versatile.

■ Candles are one of the most important of the standard supplies. We recommend you have a few pillar candles, ranging from tall to squat, taper candles (dripless is best), votive candles, and a good supply of tea candles. (Unlike votives, tea candles are contained in small metal cups, so you can drop them in any cup, glass, or bowl to transform ordinary vessels into glowing sources of light.) Amass more white and off-white candles than colored candles (you knew we were going to say that, didn't you?). Buying neutrals is especially smart when it comes to larger, pillar-style candles, because they're the most expensive and longest lasting. Tapers and votives are another story. They're inexpensive and have short lives, so collect as many colors as you have storage space to hold. Always be on the lookout for candles on sale (check the grocery stores, drug stores, and discount retailers you frequent). After the holidays is a great time to stock up.

TOP: A variety of vases
CENTER: Large urn-shaped vases
BOTTOM: Pillar candles in wooden bowls

flowers and candles
according to etiquette

■ Flowers should not have a heavy, detectable scent that competes with the food.

■ It may often be better to arrange flowers in small bouquets or float them in shallow bowls rather than combine them all into one vision-blocking bouquet.

■ Prepared hosts have an empty vase or two easily at hand, ready for the flowers guests inevitably bring.

■ Candles should be dripless and scentless, and should appear only after dark.

■ Be sure the flames of your table's candles don't meet your guests at eye level.

Small bouquets repeated down the center of the table

FIVE GREAT FLOWER TIPS

■ The colors of the flowers you choose can help set the mood. Reds and yellows are bright, energizing colors. Blues and greens are soothing and calm.

■ Your lighting choice will affect the look of your flowers. White and light yellow flowers, for example, will shimmer and glow in low candlelight, but flowers in shades of indigo and maroon will be nearly unnoticeable if the lighting isn't a bit brighter.

■ Practice seeing substitute vases everywhere: old metal buckets and baskets, vintage milk bottles, small ceramic cream pitchers, brightly colored mixing bowls, a collection of shot glasses. Even a pedestal-style cake stand makes a beautiful base for a collection of clear juice glasses filled with single buds. Cut flower stems short if you want the blooms to cascade over the sides of a shallow container. Or, stick jars of water inside a wide, deep container to hold the flower stems in place.

■ Choose flowers that echo the flavor of the meal: bright, tropical flowers to complement exotic, spicy food, say, or single, simple blossoms floating in bowls at each guest's place if the meal is cold noodles and sake.

■ If you need something to hold flower stems in place at the bottom of a clear glass vase, make the something part of the look. Try smooth, dark pebbles, colored glass chips, nuts and bolts, costume jewelry, or broken shards of pottery. If you're propping dried branches or stalks in place, options for the base include everything from nuts and berries to bird seed and wild rice.

table settings 101

AIN WINEGLASS ABOVE THE POINT OF THE MAIN-COURSE knife...fish forks on the left, but seafood forks on the right...dessert flatware set in advance; cups and saucers later...where *does* all this stuff go—and when do you put it there?

First, take comfort in the fact that proper etiquette almost always favors the simple over the unnecessarily complex. Second, take a look at the illustrations on pages 36 and 37. They pull together all the elements of a proper table setting and play them out in easy-to-imitate variations.

settings according to etiquette

■ To ensure enough elbow room for each guest, allow at least 30 inches (75 cm) from the center of one service plate to the center of the next.

■ Plates should be placed ½ to 1 inch (1.3 to 2.5 cm) from the table's edge.

■ One small set of salt and pepper shakers should be provided for every four to six guests. For added elegance, use salt cellars, tiny, shallow, open bowls filled with salt to be pinched with one's fingers or transported to food using a tiny spoon.

seating according to etiquette

■ Seat together those who have hobbies, professions, or interests in common.

■ Seat spouses apart unless it's a family gathering.

■ Male-female alternation is the common seating practice, but it's better to forego this pattern if it prevents you from pairing people with common interests.

■ A female guest of honor sits to the right of the host, a male guest of honor to the left of the hostess.

■ At a formal dinner hosted by a woman with a woman guest of honor, the two sit at opposite ends of the table. Likewise with two men.

■ Place cards are helpful at a dinner of more than eight or ten. Place them atop the napkins (if the napkins are set on the plates) or just above the plates. Clear the place cards after the first course, unless the party is so large that they're needed to help guests with identification. Hosts traditionally don't have place cards.

A FULL-BLOWN TABLE SETTING   Most of us will probably never set a table with this many pieces at each place. Still, if you know the proper setting for an elaborate, multi-course meal, you've got a starting point for scaling back. Flatware on the left of the plate (working outside in, just as a diner would) includes a fish fork, a main course fork, and a salad fork (placed this way when salad is served after the main course). On the right of the plate are a seafood fork (for a shellfish dish before the fish), a soup spoon, a dinner knife, and a salad knife. This setting could also include a fish knife just before the dinner knife and a dessert spoon and fork (which can also be brought out when dessert is served). Glasses, working from the northwest point of the diagonal down, include a water goblet, a glass for white wine (for the soup and/or fish courses), a glass for red wine (for the main course), and a glass for dessert wine. The butter knife, on the butter plate, mimics the positions of the other knives.

A SIMPLER TABLE SETTING This more typical setting is for a meal including soup, a salad, a main course, and dessert. The dessert fork and spoon are positioned above the setting, with the fork pointing right and the spoon left, as if they were simply moved up from their positions beside the plate.

A DESSERT SETTING For a setting with no knife, the fork goes on the right, inside the spoon. If this were a smaller coffee spoon rather than a standard beverage spoon, you'd place it on the saucer with the coffee cup

serving according to etiquette

You may align yourself with the French, the Russians, the Americans and English, or the restaurateurs when determining how best to serve your guests.

Standard until the mid-19th century, French service was a variation of what we might call family style today. Many dishes of food were put in the middle of the table, and it was up to the person nearest each dish to make sure everyone got a bit of what they wanted (with no one trying everything, there was simply too much food). Russian service (introduced at the Russian embassy around 1850) replaced French service, becoming all the rage in Paris and eventually elsewhere. Servers presented platters of food to seated guests, who served themselves. Formal American service (called English service by the English) calls for the host to carve the meat at the table (according to the preferences of each guest), add the vegetables, then pass plates down the table or have servers deliver them. And restaurant service involves arranging food on individual plates in the kitchen, then delivering equal portions to all.

Modern service is often a combination of the four (minus the servants), with complicated items plated in the kitchen and other platters of food placed on the table and passed among guests.

■ All dishes should be passed from the left, leaving recipients' right hands free to serve themselves.

■ Clear no more than two plates at a time, scraping and stacking them out of view of your guests.

■ Clear all plates, serving dishes, condiments, and salt and pepper shakers before dessert is served.

■ In the United States, coffee or tea is typically served with dessert. In Europe, it is more commonly served afterwards, accompanied, perhaps, by chocolate.

■ Cream and sugar are offered from the left or passed counterclockwise.

food is
the focus

first course
set piece

W HEN YOU WERE YOUNGER, YOU COULD make a scene at any table by playing with your food. Now that you're older and wiser (not to mention the host), better to create a scene of a different sort by playing *off* your food.

The concept is charmingly obvious (in a why-didn't-I-think-of-this-before sort of way). Use your first course as the springboard for a simple yet striking table decoration. Here, the first course actually *becomes* the table decoration, with hollowed-out pumpkins doubling as soup bowls. The idea is echoed with an easy center-piece arrangement of a pale pumpkin and a few meandering vines of ivy.

Want nearly effortless? Assemble a centerpiece collection of your featured ingredient, like the wire basket filled with uncooked artichokes, on the facing page. If your starting dish is spicy, try a display of dried red chilies or fresh, whole jalapeños. At a summer lunch with lemonade, maybe the centerpiece is a clear pitcher filled with bright, whole lemons.

Serve your salad in the form of edible flower buds; these are made of endive leaves tied with bright green strips of scallion. When guests slice through the tie with a knife, the endive leaves fall open to reveal the salad inside—and your table needs nothing more than a touch of candlelight to highlight the flowering first course.

endive pouch step-by-step

1. Select very fresh scallions with long green leaves. (Leeks also work well.) Peel away a few outer leaves and drop them into boiling water for 10 to 20 seconds, just until they're droopy, then immerse them in cold water.

2. Since you'll use only the large, outside endive leaves, select large heads with plenty of nice-looking leaves. Delicately remove two or three layers of leaves, saving the heart for salads or for dipping. Be careful; endive bruises easily.

3. In the palm of your hand, or in a small, shallow bowl, place two endive leaves so their bottoms overlap. Add another overlapping leaf, then in the "bowl" you've created, add the filling. We used a baby lettuce blend, which we packed in lightly. You could also use a lightly dressed crab or chicken salad, as long as it's not too solidly bound together.

4. Add more endive leaves, overlapping the bottoms, to finish creating the flower-like packet that holds the salad. Close the packet firmly (it's still in your palm), and press it shut with your fingers and thumb. If there are gaps, add more leaves to the outside until the packet is solid and closed.

5. If you can recruit some help, have your assistant wrap a scallion leaf around the packet (slightly less than halfway up) and tie a small bow while you hold the packet firmly closed. If you're on your own, hold the packet closed with a rubber band while you tie the scallion.

set off your food

A BUNCH OF ASPARAGUS WRAPPED WITH twine was all it took to inspire Manet. Monet found his muse in groupings of pears and grapes; for Cézanne, it was soup tureens and bottles of wine. As any French Impressionist will tell you, sometimes there's nothing more stunning you can put in the center of your table than the food and serving dishes themselves.

One of the best ways to turn your table into a tableau is to celebrate the shape, color, and texture of the food you're serving. Take the artistic arrangement shown here—nothing but the spare simplicity of pure white dishes heaped with some of a good meal's most essential ingredients. (Whoever said you need little more than a loaf of bread and a jug of wine was onto something.)

T HE FUN AND EASY ARTISTRY OF CREATING A food-focused composition of your own is in pairing the food and the serving pieces. Maybe it's wooden bowls, butcher-block boards, and crockery pitchers for a rustic meal of stew, bread, and cider. Or, perhaps it's splashy platters in a riotous mix of colors for a summer-time spread of tropical fruits and Caribbean dishes.

These aren't fussy settings; keeping additional accents to a minimum will make them all the more vivid and effective. You can forget everything from table coverings to flowers. Just light a few low, unobtrusive candles (short pillars are perfect), and let your guests take pleasure in how they light up the food you've put before them.

When the food is center stage, serving pieces, from platters and bowls to bread baskets and water pitchers, play
a more important (not to mention more noticeable) sup-
porting role. That makes this method of table setting a
terrific excuse for showing off heirloom favorites, great
new finds, and everything in between. It also makes a new
serving piece the only excuse some of us need
to invite a few friends for dinner.

THE URGE TO GATHER AROUND A FLAME AND FIX A meal goes *way* back. You don't need a campfire to satisfy the lingering primal impulse, just the setup for any classic dish prepared group-style at the table, from fondue to Sunday-morning waffles. The key to setting the scene for these hands-on events? Keeping the table simple and uncluttered.

If you don't start with a bit of structure, the reaching, leaning, dripping, dipping, and abundant sharing that are part of the communal charm of cooking at the table might turn to chaos—and a disorganized mess. Best to think like a choreographer when you're laying out the components, mentally working through all the moves and making sure each guest will be within easy reach of food and equipment.

cooking at the table

When diners are helping themselves to fondue, for example, they are also maneuvering their way through hot pots of boiling oil or melted cheese, dishes of food and condiments, and lots of arms, elbows, and skewers. Ideally, you want one fondue pot per four people. When it comes to the meat, bread, or fruit for dipping and the sauces or other condiments, single, heaping platters won't work nearly as well as smaller groupings of strategically placed plates.

And don't turn an already full and active table into an obstacle course by tossing in lots of burning candles and vases of flowers. Instead, press side tables into service for most of the added touches. Then, on the main table, you can incorporate clean, minimal accents, such as the ivy woven around dishes of dipping sauces here. When you've got lots of tiny dishes that go together (an array of mustards, maybe, or various chutneys), creating groupings of them on serving dishes cuts down on the confusion.

M AKE THE MAIN FEATURE OF YOUR TABLE a wok, a raclette grill, a waffle iron, or any of a number of other tabletop cookers, and you've got an automatic focal point—and a definite party.

FONDUE POT AND FORKS Considered a Swiss invention, fondue is a communal dining tradition throughout the Alpine region of Europe (and, thanks to its heyday in the 1970s, lots of other places). To fondue, you cook or heat food in either oil, broth, or cheese. Traditionally, oil and broth fondue are for cooking meat and vegetables; cheese fondue is for dipping bread and fruit. Oil or broth fondue usually makes a whole meal. Cheese fondue typically serves as a single course or as an appetizer. Fondue pots are heated by either a flame under the pot or by electricity. Electric pots are the most reliable for oil or broth fondue, because they're better at keeping the heat consistently high. In addition to meal-size fondue pots, a variety of small pots are made exclusively for chocolate. For an elegant dessert display, pair one with tiny squares of cake and fresh fruit for dipping.

RACLETTE GRILL From the same folks who brought you fondue, this Swiss tabletop cooking method is another one that lets everyone in on the act. Place chunks of Gruyere, Emmentaler, or Swiss cheese in each pie-shaped pan, then tuck them under the griddle to be melted by a broiler. On top of the grill, briefly sauté parboiled potatoes and pearl onions—and perhaps some mushrooms. Each diner rakes some sautéed vegetables onto a plate, pulls a raclette pan from the broiler, pours melted cheese over the top, then scoops up the blend with crusty bread. Raclette is traditionally accompanied by cold, crisp pickles.

If the cooking equipment you're using has to be plugged in, situate one end of the table near an outlet, and tape the cord to the floor to prevent people from tripping and pulling the cooker from the table.

TABLETOP GRILL You need good ventilation if you're grilling at the table. Porches, decks, and rooms with open windows are the best spots. Nearly anything you might cook on a traditional grill can go on a table-top grill, just in smaller portions. Kabobs or souvlakia are perfect possibilities. If you want an icebreaker and appetizer in one, set out skewers of marinated shrimp, meat, or vegetables, then let guests grill their own personalized kabobs.

WOK No, no, we're not suggesting a steaming stir-fry right in the middle of the table. But tempura—lightly battered tidbits of fish, meat, and vegetables flash-cooked in hot oil—now there's a dish perfectly suited for table-top cooking. Look for electric woks with clip-on wire racks to rest the cooked tempura on. We suggest you set out platters of butterflied shrimp; small, whole calamari; or marinated chicken. For vegetables, try thinly sliced pieces of sweet potato, thick bell pepper, onion rings, broccoli flowerets, and whole mushrooms. Find a recipe for tempura batter and set out a bowl for every two people. All you need to add is a salad, a few dipping sauces, and some long chopsticks.

clambakes, shrimp boils, and other messes

WHOLE TABLE-SETTING TRADITIONS HAVE EVOLVED out of celebrating the unavoidable mess some meals make. From newspaper-covered tables to a bountiful supply of oversized napkins, the look tells guests that the last thing they should worry about is a misplaced drop of sauce.

With the possible exception of a bucket of ice-cold beer, few things symbolize do-it-yourself, peeling-and-shucking seafood fests like aprons, bibs, napkins, and other protective gear. No need to hide these utilitarian items in the shadow of other table decorations; put 'em front and center. Plain white chef's aprons are often available for reasonable prices at craft stores; look for them with the T-shirts, ball caps, and other plain items sold for personalizing with fabric paints. You can also find them at restaurant supply stores. Roll one per guest around a nutcracker, seafood fork, napkin, and any other necessities. The tidy bundle serves as a nifty place setting. Or, it can be heaped with others in a basket on a buffet table.

Want other options? Already built to tie neatly around any neck, bandanas make great messy-meal bibs. Buy an inexpensive pack of them in assorted colors, and tie them in flamboyant knots to the back of each chair. Fluffy, white terry-cloth hand towels are the perfect stand-in for standard napkins. They not only look inviting, piled in cushy stacks next to the hot sauce and lemon wedges, they also let guests know right away that serious finger food is in store.

F EW TABLE-ETIQUETTE TRADITIONS ARE trivial; most meet some real mealtime need. So it goes with finger bowls. Invented long ago for the dainty dipping of fingertips between a finger-food course and a flatware course, this civilized piece of table-ware has a place at modern meals—especially messy ones like these. Once, only rimless glass or silver bowls would do. At a casual clambake today, small, shallow vessels of any kind are fine. Put one at each place, fill it with tepid water, and float something scented on top—geranium leaves, rose petals, and herb sprigs are all effective and eye-catching options.

Purists dump the pots of boiled shellfish, potatoes, and corn directly onto a paper-covered table. The rest of us would prefer to contain the spread a bit (not to mention protect the table surface), but we don't want to interfere with the free-for-all feel a meal like this should have. The answer: an unobtrusive, easy-to-build trough (yes, we said trough) for the middle of the table. It functions as a nearly invisible platter.

WHAT YOU NEED

2- x 2-inch (5 x 5 cm) railing (length
determined by trough size)

Four 3-inch (7.5 cm) drywall screws

Thick food-grade plastic sheeting

Drill with a ⅛-inch (3 mm) bit

Scissors

Stapler

Saw

1. Decide how large you want the trough.
It's essentially a large platter to go down
the center of the table, so allow room for
plates and condiments to fit around the
outside of the table. Our trough measured
12 x 44 inches (30.5 x 113 cm) allowing for
12 inches (30.5 cm) of space around the
outside.

2. At each corner, predrill a hole for the
drywall screw. Screw all four corners
together to make a frame, as shown.

3. Roll out a length of plastic. Cut a
piece quite a bit larger than the
trough; you'll trim off the excess
later. Lay the frame on the plastic,
and wrap the plastic around to the
backside of the frame (the side facing you). Staple the plastic onto one
long side of the frame, as shown.

4. Turn the frame over and drape the
plastic loosely into the frame. Once
it's draped into the recess, hold the
plastic tightly against the frame so it
doesn't slip, and turn the frame back
over. Staple the plastic to the back of
the frame on the other side and to
the ends, tucking the corners to
make a relatively neat fit. (Keep in
mind that this is a trough; don't
sweat it too much.) Trim away the
excess plastic. Congrats! You've
made your first food trough, we'll bet.

meals of many condiments

HOW DO YOU CREATE A SENSIBLE, IN-SYNC TABLE that also has a dash of style, when the meal (maybe make-your-own tacos or burgers with dozens of toppings) calls for lots of little dishes? Let the dilemma dictate your table decor. Pair the need to consolidate with the impulse to coordinate, adding order and ornament all at once.

One of the best ways to keep a table that's crowded with condiments from seeming cluttered is to use serving dishes that provide a unified look. Trouble is, few of us own the dozens of matching mini dishes that would make the streamlined setting possible. As the photos here show, other alternatives lie just beyond your kitchen cabinets. You can pick up a stack of terra-cotta plant saucers for about half the cost of a potted fern, then piece together a working centerpiece that's perfect for a meal with a Southwestern theme. Clear and colored glass candle saucers would work just as well for a variety of themes. And don't overlook food itself when you're in search of small, clever serving pieces. Fill hollowed-out coconuts with fruit salsa, peppers with chopped onions, dried corn husks with herbs or olives…you get the idea.

Containing the chaos is another main objective of any condiment-laden meal, whether you're dealing with all the different chutneys and yogurt sauces that go with curry, or a collection of nuts, sprouts, croutons, and dressings for a salad. Holding vessels are the answer, and, happily, the rules that govern what qualifies are few. This wooden canoe is the perfect rustic container for the toppings for a late-fall chili party. Birthday cookout for a group of six-year-olds, on the other hand? Bring on the toy tractors.

available
in season

spring

THOSE OF US WHO WEATHER LONG, barren winters are so starved for signs of life come spring, we find the subtlest ones striking. No need for bold, brilliant splashes of color and design. The elegance of a newly opened tulip or the annual wonder of buds beginning to blossom is enough.

Even the simple pleasure of spring-green grass can be elevated to centerpiece status in this season that celebrates new growth. We're all giddy enough in the pre-summertime that it doesn't yet represent the months of mowing ahead. Instead, grass symbolizes going barefoot, playing Frisbee, and lounging under trees. You can easily summon these quintessential scenes of spring with tiny tabletop gardens.

Long stainless steel pans used for plastering (inexpensive and easy to find at most home improvement stores) provide the base. Fill the pans with strips of sod or grow your grass from seed (see details on page 63), then simply water them and let them dry in a sunny windowsill before setting them in place. Add height and more life to the vernal display by poking a budding branch or two into each container, choosing branches thin enough that they don't obstruct the view from one side of the table to the other.

best blooms

Here are our top picks for blooming branches that make the transition from tree to table with style.

WITCH HAZEL brightens in late winter with fragrant and delicate yellow flowers.

FORSYTHIA buds appear well before the leaves emerge in early spring. The flowers are bright yellow.

REDBUD, also known as eastern redbud, is native to North America. It features clusters of purple-pink flowers in the spring.

FLOWERING QUINCE, native to Japan, is a favorite shrub for bonsai art. Its fragrant flowers (which can be red-orange, white, pink, or red, depending on the variety) open in late winter and early spring.

BRADFORD PEAR is a hardy tree that bears clusters of white flowers in early to mid-spring.

PLUM trees come in many varieties. Their rose-pink blossoms appear for several weeks in early spring.

WEEPING CHERRY, or any of the ornamental cherries native to Japan, bears clusters of pink, rose, and white flowers (depending on the variety) in the spring.

RIGHT: These small, contained patches of a fresh spring lawn are just the place to tuck in a symbol or two of the season's most popular hunt.

other table-worthy harbingers of spring

ASPARAGUS: tie up a bunch with raffia. The spears will last longer if you make a fresh bottom cut and display them in a shallow pan of water.

BULBS: use them to fill a wide, clear glass vase.

SEEDS: pour a bunch into a bowl, or fill a bowl with a collection of vintage seed packets if you can find some at an antique store.

an insider's guide to grass

If you're looking for tips on lawn care, that's another book. But if you want to fill a container or two for your table, here are the options.

SOD

This time of year, garden centers are stocked with strips of sod people use for putting in and patching lawns. Chances are, you can purchase just the amount you need and cut it to fit your container. An even easier option is using a sharp knife to cut a small strip (grass and a thin layer of dirt) from a corner of your yard. Simply pick a spot where it won't be too badly missed during the short period of time before it fills back in.

GROWING GRASS FROM SEED

Choose a warm-season grass seed, such as Bermuda (the variety that produces lush, green golf courses). Sow the seeds heavily on top of the soil in your container, then water them daily without oversaturating them. Your grass will do best in loose soil; soil with a high bark content provides much better drainage than potting soil. It'll also need a lot of bright light (either a grow light or direct sunlight) and warm temperatures (around 70ºF [21ºC]). Look for sprouts in about seven days and a container of grass in a couple of weeks.

ALFRESCO DINING IS LIVING AT ITS BEST— letting the breeze, the sunshine, and whatever's in bloom create the atmosphere. Yet most of us assume that eating outdoors always means picnic tables, blankets, or lawn furniture. Think again. This outdoor feast turns preconceived notions inside out— that is, inside furniture comes outside. Moving the dining room outdoors—tables and chairs, fine china, and all—has been a summer diversion among European aristocracy for hundreds of years. It was also a grand style of warm-weather entertaining in the antebellum American south.

Our modern-day version celebrates the welcome return of warm days by taking the party outdoors to the edge of a country field. A loose drape of cotton ducking sets the spot for a playful vernal celebration. The elegant look is easy when you draw on a basic color theme, as we did with our pairing of red and white: red tulips in white garden urns, strawberry compotes in white tureens, and luscious strawberry tarts on white cake plates. Pure white table linens carry the theme with vintage monogrammed napkins folded across the chair backs.

On the bench doubling as a side table in the background, a grand arrangement of spring flowers augments the newly budding trees. Next to the bench, a basket of shawls and blankets sits ready should the fickle spring winds turn chilly.

NO NATURAL OBJECT REPRESENTS the spirit of spring quite like the egg. This delicate symbol of life itself can stand up to coloring, painting, gilding, even decoupage. But, as is often the case, the most elegant form of decoration and display is also the easiest. Our centerpiece for a brunch sideboard features a generous glass compote filled with brown and white eggs dyed to the subtlest shades of pastel.

egg dyeing step-by-step

1. Blow the eggs first by poking a hole into the bottom and side of each and using a rubber ear syringe, which you can find at a pharmacy. Rinse them, and let them dry.

2. Mix your dyes in disposable cups, combining a drop or two of food coloring (we used the standards: blue, red, yellow, and green), a tablespoon of vinegar, and a cup (.24 L) of boiling water. In addition, mix a cup (.24 L) of strong tea and a cup (.24 L) of strong coffee.

3. Begin dyeing the eggs. To achieve the faintest colors, don't leave them in the dye mixture for longer than 30 seconds or so. You may want to dip some of the dyed eggs into the coffee or tea mixtures for a moment or two afterward to soften their shades.

4. Place the dyed eggs carefully into the slots in an egg carton to dry completely before you incorporate them into your centerpiece.

summer

FARMERS' MARKETS ARE IN FULL SWING, gardens are overflowing, and fruit stands are selling their wares by the bushel. If you want to dress your table with nature's bounty, there's no time like the most bountiful. Best of all, this is the season when living—and entertaining—are easy.

Even if it's been years since summertime's meant an official break for you, this season of barbecues, beach picnics, and campfire cooking is a bit of a vacation from rigid rules for everyone. Here's a beautiful case in point. Just when you thought *centerpiece* meant a single arrangement in the middle of the table, a wandering row of cream bottles filled with roses steals the show on a summer table.

Herbal centerpieces are another delightful summertime break with tradition. They can echo the flavors of the meal; maybe an arrangement of rosemary and mint if you're serving lamb, or a big bunch of basil and oregano with pasta. For added color and texture, pick herbs that are flowering (chive blossoms and lavender are a wonderful combination), or include edible flowers in the mix.

And while you're breaking all the other rules, be sure to set aside any allegiance you have to crystal vases. Kitchen pitchers, garden pots, high-sided bowls, and interesting jars can all assume a relaxed pose in the center of more casual tables.

S UMMER VACATION, AND YOU'VE BEATEN a retreat to the beach, the mountains, a river, or a lake. True, your rented cabin, cottage, or campsite isn't stocked with all of your usual tableware supplies. But you're likely surrounded by something better—the makings for terrific, seasonal settings. A relaxing stroll in your new environment is often all it takes to come up with the inspiration—and ingredients. Locate your next vacation destination on the tabletop travel guide we've created here, then use the ideas as a starting point for setting your own table away from home.

SAND makes an excellent base for everything from candles to miniature Zen gardens in the middle of the table.

CANDLEHOLDERS surround you—the right piece of driftwood, a patch of moss, or a nicely flattened rock. You can also create them from whatever glassware you've got on hand. Wine or beer bottles hold tapers, ashtrays are perfect for pillars and votives, and drinking glasses make hurricane holders that stay put and keep candles lit, even in the wind (just add a scoop of sand to the bottom before placing your candle inside).

STONES in interesting shapes make pretty weights on top of napkins when a breeze is blowing.

SHELLS have many uses. Large ones can be used as serving dishes for condiments such as lemon wedges, cocktail sauce, or olives.

VASES filled with anything you can't find at home are automatically appealing. Try sea oats, cattails, or a thorny branch of ripe berries.

pack before you go

Supply of candles of various sizes

Matches or lighter

A few vases or jars (These versatile vessels can hold both candles and flowers. You can also hit a thrift store or an antique shop when you arrive; they're inexpensive sources for vases, candleholders, and local color.)

tip of all tips

When you're on vacation, pack up a few of your favorite table-setting props to take home (sand, shells, etc.), then pull them out next January, when that summery spot seems *veeeery* far away. They'll make a perfect (and original) setting for a mid-winter meal with others who are also dreaming of a place in the sun.

autumn

AS COOLER WEATHER AND SHORTER DAYS move us inside, it's understandable that we'd want to bring a few keepsakes with us. For centuries, humans have been celebrating autumn by carrying symbols of its harvest to the table—apples, hazelnuts, branches dotted with brilliant clusters of red-orange berries, ears of drying corn. This is also the time to light our indoors with crackling fires and plenty of candlelight, just the antidote to the season's waning sun.

The fall table here is set for a relaxed yet elegant celebration of the season. Three large vases filled with nuts—one with pecans, two with chestnuts—provide enough stability to hold taper candles in place. We set small pumpkins between each vase, then encircled everything with spare strands of bittersweet.

I F HARVESTS WERE RATED FOR THEIR ROMANTIC appeal, those that take place in vineyards would top the list. Fall wine tastings are an elegant way to celebrate one of early autumn's most popular crops. Here, a few simple pieces create the perfect atmosphere. Grape vines spill out of a galvanized-metal flower bucket. They're propped in place by a large ball of chicken wire inside. To attach grape bunches to the arrangement, wrap a small strand of medium-gauge wire around the stem of each bunch, then twist the other end around the chicken wire inside the bucket. Big wooden lids used for packaging wheels of cheese make ideal serving platters. Check with the deli manager at any supermarket about extras that might be stacked up in the storeroom.

FINDING THE GRAPEVINE

In most regions, grapes indigenous to the area grow wild in surrounding woodlands. It's also not uncommon to find grapevines flourishing in suburban backyards. But if you can't easily get your hands on a few nearby vines when you want them, check with a florist about special ordering them.

wine tasting check list

WINE
A tasting of six wines makes for a relaxed pace for a two- to three-hour event. Count on two ounces (60 mL) per wine per person for the tasting itself, with enough extra so guests can go back to what they enjoyed.

FOOD
Focus on palate cleansers that won't detract from the wines: unseasoned crackers, crusty white bread, and mild cheeses.

GLASSES
All-purpose tasting glasses (narrower at the rim than in the middle of the bowl) are all you need (though serious connoisseurs may want differently shaped glasses for each type of wine). Wine merchants will often loan or rent their stemware, especially if you're buying the wine from them.

BASINS FOR EXCESS WINE
Veteran tasters say it's not necessary to swallow wine to taste it. Good news for guests who want to pace themselves. Provide small, individual cups for spitting out wine between tastes, and several larger basins (tin buckets from craft stores work well) for discarding wine from glasses.

WHITE LINENS
Examining wine's color is part of the tasting process. White napkins (and tablecloths, if you're sitting at tables) are the best backdrop.

PAPER AND PENS
The studious members of the group may want to take notes as they taste. Giving each guest a tasting list with space for writing their impressions is also a nice touch.

NOTHING SYMBOLIZES THE SEASON quite like turning leaves. What a fortunate coincidence that they also lend themselves to lots of table-setting functions.

Fan out a base layer of leaves on a plate of paté and crackers, stuffed mushrooms, or most any other sort of finger food. To set off this selection of cheeses, we picked leaves that spanned the color wheel of fall, from yellow-tipped green to crimson.

To create an elegant display that's about as fuss free as you can get, tuck a single leaf into a tall, clear wine or champagne glass at each place setting. Guests can slip out the leaves and toss them in the center of the table before drinks are poured.

You may not need place cards, but why resist when they're as effortless and enchanting as these. A metallic pen, a deciduous tree, and you're set.

THE ANCIENT CELTS, WHO WERE BIG ON AUTUMNAL ritual (they're credited with inventing Halloween, after all), never carved pumpkins to celebrate the season. They hollowed out turnips for their holiday candleholders. Reach back into the mists of time to create a fall table setting with imaginative appeal and (just when everyone else is trotting out the gold and russet) an unexpected color scheme.

turnip candle step-by-step

1. Choose three medium-sized turnips with "tails."

2. Hollow them out with a thin-edged spoon, scraping carefully until there's only a thin shell remaining.

3. Create a tripod for each by tying three large nails, also called spikes, together with twine or twisting them together with high-gauge (thin) craft wire.

4. Drop a votive or tea candle into each.

winter

THE SLANT-LIGHT GLOW OF AUTUMN is long past, and the bright, sparkly cele-brations that followed have been packed away until next year. Winter is really here now. You can finally stop for a moment, take a breath, and take refuge in a quiet, con-tented season when simplicity rules.

By the time the heart of winter sets in, tinsel and glitter have given way to the more natural brilliance of snow and ice. A sudden cold snap can capture the entire landscape in a still, frozen display—one it's easy to imitate indoors with a little help from your freezer. The ice luminary centerpiece here features cranberries and hemlock suspended in ani-mation. You can create your own out of a variety of cold-weather greens and berries, in addition to twigs, pine-cones, and vines.

WHAT HOLDS UP UNDER ICE

Hemlock

Juniper

Eucalyptus

Holly

Winterberry

Cranberries,

Pepperberry

Bittersweet

ice luminary step-by-step

1. Line a cardboard box with a small plastic garbage bag. We used a box 8 inches square by 10 inches deep (20 x 25 cm), but any size will work as long as it fits in your freezer. Press the bag into the corners, minimizing the wrinkles and folds as much as possible (though a few wrinkles will only add to the final look).

2. Hold a large can in the center of the box, aligning the top of the can with the top of the box. We used a large juice can, 4¼ inches in diameter by 7 inches tall (10.7 x 17.5 cm). Scoop ice cubes into the box until the can rests upon the cubes and is flush with the top of the box. Fill the can with rocks, so it won't float when the mold is filled with water.

3. Add greenery and berries to the space between the can and box, using a chopstick to nudge them into place. To keep all the berries from floating to the top, alternate scoops of crushed ice with sprinklings of berries.

4. Slowly fill the space between the can and the box with water, and freeze the luminary until it's solid (between 24 and 36 hours).

5. Unmold the luminary by first dumping the rocks from the inner can. Then, in the sink, fill the can with warm water until you can work it out. Finally, pull the plastic liner and the block of ice out of the box (or tear the box) to free the luminary. Remove the liner from the luminary's surface.

Display the luminary on a tray with a rim to catch the water as it slowly melts.

ONE OF THE GIFTS OF WINTERTIME is its spareness. It gently pushes us to search a little harder for bits of the season's beauty. In the process, we often see things differently. Take bare branches, for example. Back in the overgrown lushness of July, it never would have dawned on you to fill a tall, clear vase with them and call the creation a centerpiece. But come January, the stark look may strike you as so stunning, you won't be able to stop at one arrangement; we couldn't. What makes this winter table especially breathtaking is the contrast of the deep red branches and the cranberries against the rest of the snow-white setting.

choosing your pears and logs

Pears with flat bottoms will sit best on the logs.

If you have trouble getting a pear to stand upright, try this technique: hammer a small nail into the center of the log, leaving about ½ inch (1.3 cm) of the end sticking up, and anchor the bottom of the pear to that.

Look for logs with textured or colorful bark, such as cedar, birch, oak, or aspen. Lichen and moss also add interest.

Choose logs that measure roughly the same in diameter as your candles. Then use a miter saw (which provides a smooth cut) to cut the logs into sections ranging from about 2 to 5 inches (5 to 12.5 cm) long.

VARIATIONS

Top your logs with apples, pomegranates, oranges (if they've still got leaves attached, that's especially nice), or limes. Or, drill 1-inch (2.5 cm) holes into the logs to hold taper candles.

THE THERAPEUTIC VALUE OF CHOPPING WOOD was first touted by an ancient Chinese Zen master. Here's a wonderful excuse to give his advice a try—and a beautiful way to share the afterglow with guests. This easy table runner is nothing more than sections of river birch logs of varying heights topped with an alternating arrangement of pillar candles and green pears. What better way to enshrine the fruits of any season?

ORDINARY OBJECTS ASSUME A WHOLE NEW AURA in winter. A walk through the grocery store's produce section or a glance inside the refrigerator can turn up the everyday ingredients for spectacular displays. The pomegranates piled in a wooden bowl here, for example, add undeniable richness to a winter-evening dessert table.

non-
traditional
table

coffee tables
and side tables

HONEST NOW. HOW OFTEN, WHEN THERE ARE no guests around to notice, do you abandon the dining room table for a meal in the functional comfort of the living room? All those weekend bagels with the newspaper and pizzas in front of rented movies count. If you're often hap-pier eating near the couch and cof-fee table (and who  wouldn't be if that's also where the fireplace, stereo, and extra space are), there are probably casual times when others would be, too.

According to party-planning pros, it's not only acceptable but advisable when you entertain to serve a combination of purchased and homemade foods (a dessert from the bakery or appetizers from the gour-met market to complement the from-scratch soup, for example). Some of us never needed permission—and we know how to carry this concept to the extreme. For those times when the *only* homemade aspect of your event is the fire in the fireplace, cushions crowded around a coffee table can be the perfect setting. Simply add a few more dashes of decoration (the gold fabric we tossed on this table as a cloth and the red napkins are plenty) to play into the spontaneous fun of takeout.

I F YOU'RE LUCKY, YOUR FRIENDS OUTNUMBER the places at your dining room table. You can still host a bunch of them for a meal by turning coffee tables and side tables into well-set serving stations. Have appetizers on one when people arrive. Later, lay out your main course, buffet-style, on another, followed by a dessert table like the one shown here. Let guests pick up everything they need at the table (flatware, napkins, etc.), then make their way to chairs, couches, or floor cushions to eat.

organizing informality

Informal meals like these can be either charming or disorganized. Choose charm by following a few tips.

Don't scatter elements here and there. Put everything guests will need for any one course, from salt and pepper to cream and sugar, on the same table. That way, people know exactly where to go if they missed something.

Create additional table space (and nice visual appeal) by using tiered plates, baskets, pedestal-style bowls, and other containers to situate food at various levels.

Make sure you've come up with plenty of places for people to sit ahead of time; you don't want to race around looking for other options after the couch is full. Pull in extra chairs and benches, and dot the floor with throw pillows.

Since people will be balancing plates on knees, footstools, and the edges of small tables, plan foods that require as few utensils as possible.

Because your guests' laps will not be tucked safely under a table, give them generous-sized napkins to provide extra protection from crumbs, drips, and spills.

Let less is more be your mantra when it comes to table decorations. There's a lot going on at a meal like this; you want to add atmosphere, not confusion. An elegant stand of candles at the end of each table may be all you need.

pillow talk

A collection of versatile floor cushions and pillows comes in handy when you're dining around the coffee table—and they can be stacked up and put away when the party's over. You can also use furniture cushions or thick, folded blankets or quilts, and small throw rugs make perfect mats.

picnics

planning meals that move

Our highly subjective list of props that no picnic should be without:

- Blanket
- Sunscreen
- Bug spray
- Towelettes
- Flashlight
- Trash bags
- Music (homemade is preferable)
- Candles and matches
- Corkscrew
- Toy or two (Frisbee, volleyball)
- Fresh flowers (pick 'em when you get there, if possible)
- Book with good read-aloud passages

COMES A TIME EACH YEAR WHEN THE IDEA OF another indoor meal at a smooth surface supported by four legs is unthinkable. We want our feasts to move—to spots under trees, beside creeks, in open fields—anywhere with a little more breathing room. Just like those for traditional tables, picnic settings cover lots of different ground in terms of style.

This classic picnic setup (right) relies on a basket outfitted with various compartments, plus built-in holders for flatware. Colorful metal plates and plastic tumblers make sturdy tableware, and flat, stackable, plastic containers are practical serving dishes that pack up neatly.

Sometimes, a picnic setting calls for something fancier than a cooler full of sandwich fixings. Below is a classy way to transport a fully prepared meal to an outdoor concert, a social before the horse show, or your own candlelit backyard. We found this food tote at a nearby thrift store. The stackable pieces are perfect for plating whole meals. Or, you can use them as serving dishes (chicken salad in one, fresh fruit in another, and so on). A stack of bamboo steamer trays would do the same trick.

PACKING TIP

Some people believe the best picnic spots take a bit of doing to get to. While weaving, climbing, and wading your way there may add to the magic, they can make it difficult to lug a lot of baskets of breakables along. The answer? Pack the food in one backpack or two, and fill another with collapsible mess kits for serving.

I N CASE YOU HAVEN'T NOTICED, THESE BLASTS FROM YOUR past are popping up everywhere, at affordable prices and in handsome modern forms. While we're not recommending them for serving frozen dinners that come in compartmentalized aluminum containers, we *would* like to suggest that they can extend the life—and table space—of any party. Collapsible, unobtrusive, and easy to shuttle from one space to another, they're just what you need for strategically scattering drinks and appetizers around a room. They're also the answer to a too-crowded table. If an excess of platters and bottles tends to ruin the look (not to mention the traffic flow) at your table, a few well-placed stands will keep the water pitcher, the bread basket, and the salad you're serving after the soup all within easy reach, but out of the way.

TV trays and tray tables

TRAY TABLE TIP

Large cloth napkins are the perfect size for draping over standing trays. For added interest, iron the edges of a napkin while it's folded, setting neat creases that create a pattern when the napkin is laid out.

not just breakfast in bed

ALTHOUGH WE HAVEN'T conducted a scientific survey, we're guessing that, for many people, the ultimate day of leisure at home would start with breakfast in bed—and never move anywhere else. A couple of carefully stocked baskets create a setting that supports a long stay. Pack one with the right foods (easy to contain, not excessively crumbly, fine for eating with fingers). Add a thermos of coffee or tea, a bottle of water or juice, and a few pieces of fruit. Fill a second basket with all the other supplies you'll need (crossword puzzle, cordless phone, television remote, and that book you've been meaning to get back to). Position your two baskets within easy reach, and bed can be the best place imaginable for a meal, a morning, or an entire day.

FOODS FOR IN-BED DINING—ANYTIME

Breakfast

- Glazed doughnuts
- Fruit kabobs

Lunch or Dinner

- Stuffed grape leaves
- Smoked oysters
- Takeout sushi

Midnight Snack

- Peanut butter and jelly sandwiches (cut into easy-to-manage squares)
- Chocolate-covered strawberries

trays

I F , MORE AND MORE, WHEN YOU'RE entertaining people with food and drink, you find yourself beginning sentences with phrases such as *Help yourself to a...* and *Be sure to try some of the...*, then you need a setting that supports your script. Which doesn't necessarily mean you need a traditional table. Could be, a collection of trays is just the substitute you're searching for.

Let's face it. Lots of times it seems more doable (and simply more fun) to invite people to mingle over cocktails and finger foods than to lay out a formal setting (gravy boat, place cards, and all). Trays are as flexible and adaptable as stand-up events themselves. Better yet, they lend themselves to lots of creative setting combinations. So, if the majority has migrated to the deck, or guests are gravitating toward the fireplace, you can snatch up the treats and follow the crowd. The party's portable.

Here we converted a tiered plate rack into a classy hors d'oeuvre stand. It makes maximum use of counter space, puts lots of options within easy reach of any nearby guest, and contrasts nicely with the single-level, do-it-yourself bar tray beside it.

tray chic

If you want to build up a versatile collection of trays, keep an eye out for styles beyond traditional silver rounds.

- Carved wooden trays
- Old hotel service trays
- Brightly painted trays from the tropics
- Twig trays
- Trays in the shapes of flowers and foods
- Wide-rimmed vintage tin trays printed with product logos
- Trays made for specific foods (cheese, for example, or butter)
- Pedestal-style cake stands (great for stacking on top of one another)
- Compotes (long-stemmed shallow bowls)

O NE OF THE MAIN ADVANTAGES OF TRAYS over traditional tables is that they're so much easier to mix, match, and, of course, stack. Here, a shallow metal pan serves as the base tray, a clear glass cake stand sits inside it, and a silver-rimmed glass plate rests on top of that. The three-layer setup is simple. The effect: elegant.

Add accents that are striking yet uncomplicated, like the tiny votives shown here, or maybe a single red bloom on a tray of white cheeses.

Trays can carry their own weight at buffets, too. Set them, stack them, then let each guest take one and fill it up with food. The people at your party will appreciate having a substantial place to set their food and drink.

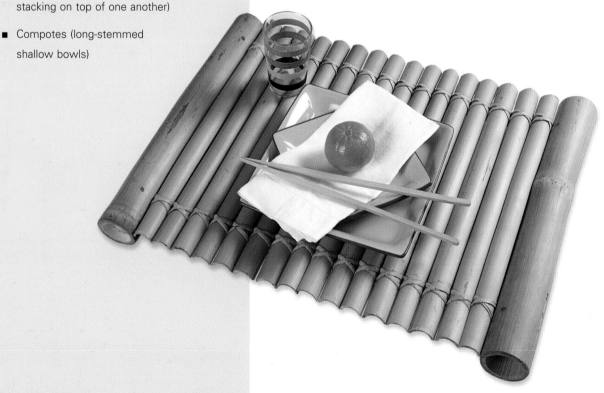

renovation party

THE PARTY IS SET FOR THIS COMING Friday. Your house (or storefront or new studio) still resembles a construction site. Lucky you. Necessity being the mother of invention and all, you've got the makings for one of the coolest housewarmings ever.

Rather than fold up the ladder, haul away the sawhorses, and stash the drop cloths, furniture pads, and other stuff out of sight, we turned them into central elements of a playful setting. The key to making your own event just as imaginative is going with what you've got. Here, a couple of sawhorses and a piece of plywood make a fine table. Beside it, a yet-to-be-installed sink does temporary duty as a bar. (Big plastic buckets or metal trash cans would work well, too; just be sure to clean them well first.) We decided a toolbox, with all of its handy compartments, would make a great holder for flatware, napkins, and condiments such as salt and pepper. And in lieu of installed lighting, we used clip lights and candles. Rig up similar candleholders by drilling 1-inch (2.5 cm) holes in lumber scraps (don't drill all the way through the wood). Then, use spring clamps to hold the scraps in place on ladder rungs, or place longer scraps drilled with multiple holes on tables.

outdoor impromptu

FURNITURE—THAT'S IT! YOU KNEW THERE was *something* missing from your back yard setup. A big, broad picnic table, maybe, for the grilled corn and the chicken. And a few small patio tables to hold all the plates, glasses, drinks, and desserts.... Don't let the lack of standard serving surfaces hold up your party plans. Improvisation is a big part of the enchantment of eating and drinking out in the open.

There's a surefire way to come up with a setting exactly like the one in your dining room: stay in the dining room. If, on the other hand, you'd prefer to make a big shady tree, a garden path, or the view from your urban terrace an integral part of the atmosphere, transform whatever you've got into a one-of-a-kind table setting.

Here, we positioned a door across the corner of a deck railing to create a delightful makeshift buffet table. Put the plates and all the fixings for whatever is cooking on the grill at one end of the deck. Rig up another table at the other end for the lemonade pitcher and the ice cream churn.

D ON'T OVERLOOK YOUR LOCATION'S natural tables: tree stumps, rock outcroppings, you name it. If it's lower than waist high and relatively level, you've got a table with far more character than anything you could haul out from inside.

And yes, we know. Wheelbarrows are for moving dirt—ordinarily. Most of us spend much of our lives following rules. Perhaps that's why sidestepping a few of them once in a while can be such a gratifying delight.

other tool shed table setting ideas

If you're using gardening containers for food, line them with parchment paper first. Use pinking shears to give the paper a decorative edge that extends beyond the rim of the container. And be sure to sterilize any tools before using them as serving utensils.

- Planters as serving dishes

- Spades and hand shovels as serving spoons

- Watering cans as pitchers

- Plant labels as place cards or to identify the food

- Metal toolbox as holder for flatware and napkins

- Window boxes full of bottles on ice

- Three-inch (7.5 cm) clay pots as votive candle holders (Or, how about floating candles in the birdbath?)

- Garden cart as a serving station

FLUE PIPES AND BOARDS CAN QUICKLY BE configured into spontaneous side tables like the one above. So can oversized terra-cotta flowerpots. Flip one upside down to form the base, then place a square piece of board or a large ceramic tile on top for the table surface. These small, temporary tables are perfect for holding plates of appetizers, bottles of wine, or bouquets of flowers.

Flowerpots can also be just the outdoorsy vessel you need to hold napkins, flatware, even food. They're less expensive than most traditional serving dishes, and they come in lots of colors, shapes, and sizes.

a reason
to celebrate

new year's day

NEW RESOLUTION, NEW CALENDAR, AND all that dancing last night—there's so much to celebrate once January 1 dawns. This one-day winter festival is often commemorated with much coming, going, and group-style sharing of food and drink. Here are some options for keeping up with it all if the crowd is convening at your place.

Before adding a top layer of shimmery, white fabric, we draped our buffet table in two shades of blue fabric, then added a meandering string of white lights. Straight pins are handy for tacking the lights in place along the setup's multiple levels.

No fancy equipment required for building up elevated areas on the table.

Cake stands, stacks of books, upside-down stock pots, even small plant stands become striking pedestals once they're covered with tablecloths, lights, and food.

tips on typical new year's day settings

POTLUCKS

It's a good idea to impose some general order in terms of setting, even if you're not responsible for making much of what's being served. Have designated places on the food table (or perhaps even separate tables) for salads, side dishes, desserts, and so on. Then, help guide what goes where as the food arrives.

Have extra serving utensils ready to go. A few extra serving dishes of various sizes and types are a good idea, too. *Do you have something I can put this on?* is one of the most commonly asked questions when people show up with their potluck contributions.

Consider a twist: making everything *but* the food potluck. Depending on the size of the party and the state of your own china cabinet, maybe what you're really short on is dishes, flatware, and glasses. You can either have a few friends help by loaning their own sets (especially if you know that one person's plates, for example, will coordinate perfectly with another's). Or, ask each guest to bring a complete place setting, then put them all out and let everyone choose someone else's to use for the meal.

BUFFETS

Make sure your table has a none-too-subtle undercurrent of liveliness; this is, after all, a party. Strategically placed noisemakers, streamers, and sprinklings of confetti are all in order. Just be sure they don't disguise what's edible or prevent guests from easily getting to it.

Could be crab dip. Or maybe deviled ham? Put out simple, hand-lettered labels for any dish that isn't easily recognizable. The plain side of a business card folded in half lengthwise makes a perfect little table tent.

If you're having quite a few friends over (more than a dozen, say), situate your table so that people can make their way through the buffet from two sides. Place plates at the starting point on each side and flatware at the end, then make sure all platters and bowls are reachable from either side and that there are two serving spoons in each.

Use serving pieces of various heights. And elevate some of your platters by placing them on top of bases (wooden blocks painted in metallic colors and the glass blocks you buy at home improvement stores are both appropriately festive without being obtrusive).

BARS

Above all, bars, like buffets, need to be accessible, especially if guests will be serving themselves. Don't stick a tiny table in a corner that's likely to get crowded (or feel claustrophobic). It's best if the bar table is open on three sides—or, better yet, round.

If you're serving just one or two types of cocktails mixed up in batches and offered in pitchers or carafes (Bloody Marys and mimosas, maybe, for a daytime buffet like the one shown here), you can really play up the theme. Go all out with tiered serving trays displaying all the traditional garnishes (celery stalks, hot sauces, horseradish, etc.).

To serve more of a variety but still keep it fairly simple, put out the four basic liquors (Scotch, bourbon, vodka, and gin) and a limited assortment of standard mixes and garnishes. Set the rest of the table with an ice bucket and tongs, jiggers, a sharp knife and a small cutting board (if the garnishes aren't already cut), and short and tall drink glasses.

A clever (and space-saving) way to add beer, wine, and champagne to the spread is to place two large ceramic plant pots or garden urns on the floor on each side of the bar, fill them with ice, then load them with bottles, so guests can help themselves. Be sure to add wineglasses, a bottle opener, and a corkscrew to the table, and put saucers under the pots to catch any condensation created by melting ice.

valentine's day

THIS IS A DAY DEVOTED TO LAVISH demonstrations of affection: not one rose, dozens; not a piece of chocolate, boxes full. It's definitely not a holiday you want to underdo. Here's a way to make sure your table gets in on the more-is-more spirit of things.

COLOR SCHEME

The effect is striking, the strategy simple. All you do is pick a color—and play it up. It can be as easy as swinging by the thrift store and picking up the cranberry glass plates you've had your eye on for weeks, borrowing your best friend's rose-colored platter, and pulling out the glasses with the ruby stems that you bought at a garage sale last summer.

Perfectly matching all your pieces isn't the objective here. Making an impact is. To come up with eight place settings, we mixed pink Depression glass, china rimmed with burgundy and salmon, and vintage state plates printed with cranberry-colored images. Deep red water glasses, a mixture of clear and cut-glass champagne flutes, and pink and burgundy napkins complete each setting. In the center of the table, we used inexpensive florist's vases as hurricane candleholders (the textured glass casts interesting light), then added red votive holders as accents. We topped the kitschy thrift-store soap dish with paper flowers.

NAPKIN RINGS

If you can twist wire, you can make these whimsical napkin rings. For each, you'll need approximately 3 feet (.9 m) of high-gauge (thin) silver craft wire. Cut off a 1-foot (.3 m) piece, shape the end into a small heart, then twist back over the heart shape several times, leaving a small tail at the base of the heart. Twist the remaining 2 feet (.6 m) of wire into a circle approximately 2 inches (5 cm) in diameter. With the wire tail you left on the heart, attach it to the top of the ring.

halloween

SOME HOLIDAY GATHERINGS CALL FOR A KIDS' TABLE, a magical little oasis where stiff chairs and stuffy conversation are banned. Halloween, however, can be a time to seat the kids in the center of the action, making their table *the* table—a place where decoration and things to do are often one and the same.

Brightly colored plastic and paper products are perfectly at home at a meal where caramel apples and candy corn are likely to top the menu. The evening's Halloween hyper-fun starts the second the kids walk in. Greet the revelers with the flash-zip-zip of an instant camera, capturing each in full spooky regalia. Then, place the pics on popcorn ball place card holders, so every kid has a spot staked out at the table. It's as easy as twisting a fat, fuzzy pipe cleaner into the shape of a curlicue and punching it into a cellophane-wrapped popcorn ball.

These "pumpkins" made from paper sacks are centerpieces, party favors, and a perfect no-mess, keep-'em-busy activity all in one.

paper sack pumpkins step-by-step

1. Fill brown paper lunch sacks with tricks and treats, one sack per guest.

2. Fold the flap down at the top of each sack, and punch a hole in the center of the fold. Use lengths of green pipe cleaner to create "stems." Insert the pipe cleaner in the hole, knot one end to hold it in place, and twist the other end into a standing spiral.

3. Attach orange, self-adhesive felt to one side of each sack. We cut our felt into shapes that resemble rectangles with slightly rounded sides.

4. Out of black, self-adhesive felt, cut out small triangles, circles, squares, and other shapes that can be used to make pumpkin faces. Put the shapes in little dishes (our French onion soup crocks, left, make ideal cauldrons).

5. Let the "carving" contest begin, with each child attaching a face to the pumpkin sack he or she will take home. And remember, NO PEEKING inside the bags!

F OR AS LONG AS WE HUMAN BEINGS HAVE BEEN growing food, we've been gathering with family and friends at the end of the season to celebrate the fruits—and vegetables—of our labors. Today, most of us harvest those fruits, vegetables, and all of their accompaniments from the shelves of well-stocked supermarkets. Still, when we come together to give thanks, we want our tables to reflect the true spirit of the season.

harvest celebration

SETTING THE TABLE WITH HARVEST IMAGES

Few celebrations conjure as many enduring images as harvest. That's why table settings in honor of this time of year don't have to be full of elaborate details. A few carefully chosen textures, symbols, and touches can set the mood immediately.

WOOD, PEWTER, AND HEAVY EARTHENWARE say fall more than delicate china when it comes to plates and serving dishes. Set out any vintage pottery you may have—even if it's cracked and stained with age.

HAND-LOOMED NAPKINS and table runners add a homespun feel you don't get with crisp linens. You can even cut napkins and hot pads out of a soft, loose-weave burlap, like we did here. Just cut the burlap exactly on the weave, then remove four or five strings from each side.

OLD-FASHIONED OIL LAMPS are in order for this homey celebration. Period outdoor lanterns and small votives placed in vintage canning jars would also create an appropriate glow.

DRY LEAFY BRANCHES and a bowl of apples take the centerpiece options beyond standard bouquets of flowers. Choose from an endless variety of natural materials that bring fall to the table—from gourds and Indian corn, to feathers and seed pods.

harvest sheaf centerpiece step-by-step

1. Cut a rectangle of florist's foam to the size you want for your centerpiece. Ours measures 3 x 3 x 9 inches (7.5 x 7.5 x 23 cm).

2. Use purchased dried wheat stalks (available at craft stores) to cover the foam block. First, fill in what will be the top surface of the centerpiece. Poke the stalks into the foam, working from the middle out, until the top surface is full of standing wheat stalks. (You'll want to poke these stalks in far enough so that they are even in height with those you'll attach to the sides of the block in step 5. It may be easiest to cut the stalks for this step before poking them in, so you have to stick them in only an inch [2.5 cm] or so.)

3. Lay the rest of the wheat stalks out in a long, flat row.

4. Wrap the sides of the foam block with double-stick carpet tape.

5. Press the taped block onto the wheat, one side at a time, so the stalks stick to the tape.

6. Attach wheat stalks, one by one, to any area where they did not stick in step 5.

7. Wrap thin craft wire around the sheaf of wheat, and tighten it to hold the stalks in place.

8. Wrap raffia around the wire and tie it in place with a bow.

9. Slip in additional wheat stalks anyplace where foam is visible.

YOUR URBAN COMMUTE INVOLVES A train or a freeway. You never see a single sheaf of wheat, no matter how diligently you scan the landscape. But you know exactly what one looks like. More to the point, you know it's the quintessential symbol of the season. Good news: these harvestime icons are almost as easy to make in centerpiece form as they are to call up in your mind's eye. We accented ours with gold-colored wineglasses and a persimmon at each place.

christmas

YOU'RE HUSTLING. YOU'RE BUSTLING. YOU'RE MOVING as fast as you can. You're also caught in that traditional holiday tug-of-war: so much to do, so little time and money. It's a season when we naturally want to entertain, but pulling off a full-blown party isn't always in the cards. What could be more low-pressure and relaxing than inviting a group to take tea—with a twist?

Our tea setup is devoid of a silver tea service and starched linen napkins, yet there's no question that it's a special affair. And with only a few easy (and hardly overdone) touches, it's quite obviously Christmassy. At last! A holiday event real people can pull off in the midst of real life. The dishes are everyday, but happen to feature a light cranberry color, which is highlighted by the burgundy-and-white napkins. Plates with dark green or icy blue details could work just as well. A few plain white cake plates add height to the display. Christmas balls that echo the colors on the plates are grouped in random collections around the table, and everything is accented by votives in bubble-glass holders and two tall tapers in the back (they're in their own holders that have been placed inside large vases filled with water and floating bay leaves). It all makes for a high-tea appearance with a low investment of effort.

CHRISTMAS REVELERS INVENTED THE CONCEPT OF more being merrier. Happily, the notion can apply not only to how many you gather around your holiday table, but to how you dress it up for the big feast. Here's your excuse to trot out your collection of lots and lots of… nearly anything…and put it center stage.

These vintage Santa boots we borrowed from a friend are an appropriately kicky focal point for a Christmas dinner. We walked them out from the center on a bed of spun fiberglass, then wound old-fashioned red and white Christmas lights around the arrangement. If you want a similarly playful look, consider using anything from snow globes to toy train cars in place of the boots. Or, go for an entirely grown-up effect—maybe glass prisms or tiny silver bells.

TWO WAYS TO ADD LIGHTS TO THE TABLE

Easiest of all: use a table with leaves. Tape an extension cord to the underside of the table, then attach the lights and pull them through the small gap where the leaves meet.

If you don't have a table with leaves, use two tablecloths, overlapping them several inches (cm) at the center. Tape an extension cord up one table leg, and run it from a corner of the table diagonally across the table, under the tablecloth that overlaps on top. At the place where the two tablecloths meet, attach the lights to the extension cord.

In either case, be sure to seat yourself nearest the place where the extension cord is taped to the floor and runs to an outlet.

place card step-by-step

1. Tie a 6-inch (15 cm) piece of gold mesh, wire-edged ribbon to the base of a Christmas light bulb.

2. Cut a 3- x 2-inch (7.5 x 5 cm) rectangle from a heavy index card, taper one corner, and punch a hole in that corner.

3. Write the name with a gold metallic marker.

4. Thread the ribbon on the bulb through the place card, then bend it and loosely crimp it.

COLLECTIONS WE'D LIKE TO SEE RUNNING DOWN THE CENTER OF A TABLE

Cocktail shakers

Old-fashioned wooden blocks

Toy cars and trucks

Plastic figures used for cake decorating

Old croquet balls

Small baskets or boxes, some opened with candles and flowers inside

Nutcrackers

P ART CANDELABRA, PART CHRISTMAS tree, all elegant modern twist. If you've had enough of the holly berries, the evergreen boughs, the balls, the bows, and the tinsel, sweep it all aside and light your late-night dessert buffet with this contemporary, coiled-copper table tree.

coiled-copper table tree
step-by-step

WHAT YOU NEED

½-inch-diameter (1.3 cm) wood dowel cut to desired height (Ours is 2½ feet [.77 m] tall.)

12-inch-diameter (30 cm) round wood base, ½ inch (1.3 cm) thick

Metallic silver spray paint

Wood screw, 2 inches (5 cm) long

12 feet (3.6 m) of ¾-inch (1.9 cm) copper tubing

13 brass Christmas tree candle holders, with rotating candle cups

Christmas tree candles

Drill and bits up to ¾ inches (1.9 cm)

Saw

Hacksaw or tubing cutter

1. Mark a spot ¾ inch (1.9 cm) from the top of the dowel, and drill a hole that matches the diameter of the copper tubing. Start with a small bit and work your way up to the required width to avoid cracking the dowel.

2. Drill pilot holes into the bottom of the dowel and through the center of the wood base. Again, start with smaller bits and work your way up.

3. Spray paint the base and dowel with metallic silver paint.

4. Fasten the dowel to the wood base with the wood screw.

5. Pick a point approximately ½ inch (1.3 cm) from the edge of the base and drill a ¾-inch-diameter (1.9 cm) hole at an angle to the base. The copper tubing will be anchored in this hole.

6. Wind the copper tubing into a tight and flat coil.

7. Take the end of the tubing that is in the center of the coil and insert it through the hole near the top of the dowel. Pull the rest of the coil down and stretch it out to conform to the width of the base. Note where the tubing meets the base, and cut the tubing accordingly. Insert the remaining end of the tubing into the hole in the base to secure it.

8. Arrange the brass candle holders in an alternating fashion around the copper tubing. Do not place the candle holders directly above or below each other (the direct heat from a burning candle could melt the base of a candle above it). Adjust the copper tubing to create space where you need it.

contributing consultants

TEX HARRISON and her husband, Tom, have owned Complements to the Chef for more than 15 years. Located in Asheville, North Carolina, Complements, as many locals call it, is a complete kitchen and entertaining store. "Brimming with the wonderful, incredible, amazing, eclectic, practical, exotic, stupendous, unequalled, fantastic, and exciting," the store has received national recognition in food and business publications. Three years ago, Complements launched an extensive website enabling customers from around the world to receive the same great personalized service enjoyed in the store.

Complements to the Chef
374 Merrimon Avenue
Asheville, NC 28801
1-800-895-CHEF
www.complementstothechef.com

SUSAN KINNEY is a designer specializing in eclectic interiors, glass and clay jewelry, fabric and rug design, and computer generated artwork. She attributes the Oriental influence in many of her designs to many years of living in Japan and Hawaii. The email address for her interior design business in Asheville, North Carolina, is SuezenDesigns@home.com

MARK ROSENSTEIN has been the chef-owner of The Market Place in Asheville, North Carolina, since 1979. He also spends time as a consultant, gardener, and author. His food fantasy is to serve the first meal/banquet to extraterrestrial life.

acknowledgments

When we get around to throwing a beautifully set dinner party to thank all those who contributed to this book by loaning tableware, opening their homes to photo shoots, and providing many other forms of assistance, here's who we'll invite.

THANKS ONE AND ALL!

Molly Bryant

April Carder

Dawn Cusick

Mike, Carol, and Ben Davis

Thom Gaines

Mary Green

Dana Irwin

Susan Kieffer

Kate Mathews

Celia Naranjo and Chris Blair

Antoine Peterson

Rob Pulleyn

Kathy Sheldon
and Claire Solomon

Heather Smith

Catharine Sutherland

Carol Taylor

Terry Taylor

Suzanne J.E. Tourtillott

Peppi White

Hugh and Sue Wingard

The staffs of
Complements to the Chef
and Pier 1 Imports

special thanks

S KIP WADE, creative coordinator, kept everything on track, on schedule, and on budget. He assembled (and often designed) the book's projects, gathered and kept track of its massive cast of props, and set up many of its photographs. We could not have created a book of this scope without him.

Skip makes a living making people and places look good. Specializing in fashion and domestics, he works in both still photography and film as a photo stylist, prop master, wardrobe manager, and location scout. He and his partner live in Asheville, North Carolina, where they're continually renovating a 1920s house. He loves good food, good wine, hiking, and puttering in the yard.

index

At-table cooking, 48–51
Autumn settings, 72–77

Bars, 110
Breakfast in bed, 94–95
Buffets, 110

Candle etiquette, 34
Candle basics, 31–32
Centerpiece basics, 31–32
Christmas settings, 120–124
Clambakes, 52–55
Coffee table settings, 87–89
Condiments, settings for, 56–57

Dinnerware basics, 13–15
Dinnerware etiquette, 15

Finger bowls, 54
First-course settings, 40–43
Flatware basics, 20–22
Flatware etiquette, 23
Flower etiquette, 34
Flower basics, 31–34
Fondue settings, 48–50

Glassware etiquette, 19
Glassware basics, 17–19

Halloween settings, 114–115
Harvest celebration settings, 116–119

Napkin basics, 25–29
Napkin etiquette, 29
New Year's Day settings, 108–111

Outdoor settings, 102–105

Picnic settings, 90–91
Place cards, 76 and 123
Potlucks, 110

Raclette grills, 50
Renovation settings, 100–101

Seating etiquette, 36
Serving etiquette, 37
Serving dishes, 46–47
Setting etiquette, 36
Side table settings, 87–89
Spring settings, 60–67
Summer settings, 68–71

Table covering basics, 25–29
Table covering etiquette, 29
Tabletop grills, 51
Tray tables, 92–93
Trays, 96–99

Valentine's Day settings, 112–113
Winter settings 78–83

Woks, 51